S|

TABLE OF CONTENTS

Unless otherwise indicated, all Scripture quotations are taken from the King James Version of the Bible.
Secrets of the Journey, Volume 3
ISBN 1-56394-061-2/B-94
Copyright © 1997 by Mike Murdock
All publishing rights belong exclusively to Wisdom International
Publisher/Editor: Deborah Murdock Johnson
Published by The Wisdom Center · 4051 Denton Hwy. · Ft. Worth, TX 76117
1-817-759-BOOK · 1-817-759-0300
You Will Love Our Website..! WisdomOnline.com

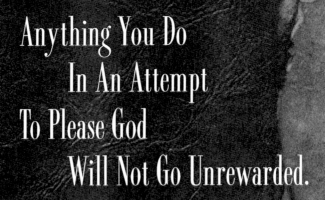

Anything You Do
In An Attempt
To Please God
Will Not Go Unrewarded.

-*MIKE MURDOCK*

～ 1 ～

LEARN TO BLESS THE LORD AT ALL TIMES

Praise Creates Internal Enthusiasm.

It is 8:35 a.m. this Thursday morning. Went to bed about 3:00 a.m. this morning. Was awakened about twenty minutes ago to a pounding in my spirit of the song, *I will bless the Lord at all times...His praise shall continually be in my mouth.*

This is one of the secrets of the journey.

You must learn continuous thankfulness.

The evil forces, the demonic spirits have one desire. Satan wants to rob God of *any moment of pleasure.* Every moment that praise does not exude and flow from my mouth, it is a *theft,* robbing God of what is rightfully His.

1.   YOU Must Personally Bless The Lord.

Nobody else can do it for you. You must praise Him.

2.   You Must Bless The Lord.

You must purpose in your heart.   Make a decision. *Determine* to do it. Become tenacious and persistent about it. Set your mind in agreement with it.

3.   You Must BLESS The Lord.

He has blessed you! Everything around you

reflects blessing. His health and healing flow through your being. Your mind throbs with motivation. Your heart is full of dreams and goals.

He is worthy of your blessing Him...honoring Him...bringing Him glory.

4.   You Must Bless THE LORD.

Many request attention. Others pull at your strength, attention, your life, your time and your energy.

Letters would get thrust in my mother's face... "Make sure Dr. Murdock gets this personally." Telephone calls came to my parents in the middle of the night. "Tell Dr. Mike this for me."

But I refuse to permit anybody around me *to become the priority focus of my life.* I was created for Him...FOR Him. When He dominates my life, *only then* do I have something worthwhile to give to *them,* minister to *them* and feed *them.* If I permit others to become mere parasites in my life, they will not be sustained. *Both of us* would be destroyed.

But if God is my focus, everything else *I do will multiply and prosper.* Others will increase also.

You must bless THE LORD. He is the precious Holy Spirit who walks besides you. Your Advisor and Counselor. Your Best Friend. The One who knows all things. He *remembers* every word that Jesus spoke, and He *reminds* you so that you can "enter into the life of Christ."

It will not always be easy. Others may *always attempt* to be the focus. They need attention. They require fueling and energy from you.

They may interpret withdrawal as rejection. Yet, you must become so conscious that if God is not your focus, your mind *loses* its peace. Your heart *loses* its joy. Your life *loses* precision and sense of purpose.

5. You Must Bless The Lord AT ALL TIMES.

How easy it would seem if you could simply "segment a part of the day" and give Him total focus, and then move on with your tasks. But there is something about the currents of this life. *The Whirlpool of Busyness.* Satan won't let you have a special time to "get alone with God" *without a fight.*

Nobody else around you will permit it either.

The very ways of this world keep you sucked in, emptied out, and with no time to simply focus on Him and His presence.

Here is your solution. *Bless the Lord at all times.*

Every moment. Each hour. Every day. Make the precious Holy Spirit your total focus and your obsession. Others will simply get the *overflow* of His flowing in your life.

AT ALL TIMES. When you are looking at contracts to sign from a realtor, whisper His name, say quietly, "I love You, precious Holy Spirit." Pray in tongues over and over continuously. "But ye, beloved, building up yourselves...praying in the Holy Ghost," (Jude 20).

AT ALL TIMES. When you are shaving and trying to get things together in the morning to head to work, do not wait until you get into your private place of prayer. Bless Him *at all times.*

You see, when your own dreams and goals become your focus, agitation will erupt. When you are thwarted, someone slows you down or does not follow an instruction, you may become disoriented.

When *others* become your focus, you may become sickened inside when their words wound you. Their countenance may show disdain and contempt for you. They may appear to have been "disappointed in you" because you failed to fulfill their secret expectations of you.

The precious Holy Spirit must become your total focus.

Friend, you cannot "leave" the road and head down a winding path to accommodate every emotional scar and the emptiness of others.

You must *stay with God.*

When you stay with God, *the Hungry* for God *will find you also.*

When you stay with God, *the Thirsty* will observe you and *fellowship will begin.*

BLESS HIM AT ALL TIMES.

It's one of the Secrets of the Journey.

RECOMMENDED INVESTMENTS:
The Holy Spirit Handbook, Vol. 1 (Book/B-100/153 pages/$15)
Where Miracles Are Born (Book/B-115/32 pages/$7)
The Holy Spirit Handbook (CD/CDS-29/$30)

≈ 2 ≈

Use Equipment Or Machines To Do A Job Whenever Possible

Proper Equipment Increases Your Productivity. Never have someone do a job that a machine can do instead. This is a little humorous explanation of the advantages of proper machines.

10 Advantages of Using Equipment

1. Machines don't *require coaxing,* just repair.
2. Machines don't get *discouraged* when their mother-in-law comes to town.
3. Machines are never *disloyal,* discussing your secrets with everyone else.
4. Your machines will not *file grievance* reports against you when you fail to meet their expectations.
5. Machines do not require *medical insurance,* sick leave or time off.
6. Machines can be *replaced* quickly and easily without breaking your heart.
7. Machines do not *request a retirement fund* and want to be paid for the years ahead when they don't perform.
8. Machines never come to work *late* and want to *leave early.*

9. Machines will work *through* lunch, requiring no "break time."

10. Machines never interrupt the productivity of *other machines,* slowing down the entire project.

That's why I continuously instruct my staff:

1. *Find the most effective equipment possible to do your present job.*

2. *Telephone other businesses or ministries to locate appropriate or needed machines and equipment.*

3. *Attend seminars and workshops that increase your efficiency or skills on computers and other machines.*

4. *Tell me what you need to do your job more efficiently, more accurately and quickly.* (I will do anything possible to make the hours of my employees more effective and productive.)

5. *Continuously evaluate your work.* What is slowing you down? What machine could make a big difference in the completion of your daily tasks and responsibilities?

6. *Present me with options, costs and potential benefits of purchasing more machines.*

Your staff will treasure it and learn to appreciate their own work load reduction because of it. It decreases the opportunities for mistakes. It increases your sense of progress and accomplishment.

Search for appropriate equipment to accomplish your tasks quickly.

It's one of the Secrets of the Journey.

≈ **3** ≈

LEARN FROM THE BEST, NOT ONLY THE ACCESSIBLE

Advisors Are Everywhere.

But you need to pursue the qualified, not the available. "A wise man will hear, and will increase learning; and a man of understanding shall attain unto wise counsels," (Proverbs 1:5).

Recently, a young pastor was discussing his difficulties with me. His ministry seemed to be a collection of tragedies and disappointments.

"Who is your mentor?" I suddenly asked.

He stumbled around a bit. He seemed uneasy and uncomfortable. So I persisted.

"Well, there is a preacher that I talk to occasionally in the next town," he answered.

"Is he truly effective?" I asked.

"No, not really. But, he is someone to talk to," was his defensive reply.

I insisted that he needed a worthy *mentor.* A *capable* mentor. Someone who knew what they were talking about.

"Would *you* consider becoming my mentor?" he asked.

"I am not even a pastor! Besides I am too busy with my own Assignment of writing, speaking and traveling. But you need to learn from someone who is the *best* at what they do—*pastoring."*

I connected him to two friends of mine who are very effective pastors. You see, it is not enough to receive advice. It is not enough to have a mentor.

You can only learn the best from the Best.

When you want to improve your game of Ping-Pong, you must play someone who is *better* than you.

When you want to increase, you must sit at the feet of someone who *knows more* than you.

Yes, it can be *intimidating.*

It is usually *uncomfortable.*

But it guarantees increase.

It is the Road to Greatness.

Most simply want someone who is accessible and *within reach.* But it is more important to *pursue the qualified, not merely the available.* When I hire an attorney, I do not want someone who is merely inexpensive or near my home. I want someone who truly cares, has proven themselves in court and is known for their thoroughness of preparation.

Some attend a church because it is near their house. How ridiculous! That's like marrying a man because he lives closer to your house than other men.

Make the investment of time. Search for those who have established their reputations and standards as *the highest.*

If you want to help a small church, find out *who* is mentoring the young pastor of that church. When he sits at someone's feet who is skilled, *you* will receive the benefits. If he is unteachable, you will taste the bitterness of every mistake and wrong decision he makes. There are hair salons close to my house. But I drive further to the young man who is the best. He does it right. He listens to me. He is not merely accessible.

Those who pursue convenience will never taste the heights of excellence.

If you are willing to inconvenience yourself in the pursuit of excellence, you will create the most remarkable and uncommon life you have ever imagined.

Don't purchase clothes simply because they are "on sale." Purchase clothes that present you *properly,* make you *feel* wonderful, and make you want to wear them *every day* of your life. I never purchase anything that I will wear only once. I want the best out of everything that I invest in.

Learning from the Best may require your willingness to live on a lower income right now.

A pastor picked me up from the airport recently. He told me something interesting about his son. His son had accepted a job at a much lower salary with another pastor. The reason? That specific pastor, though he paid a lower salary, was a superb *mentor.* His own success was remarkable. The young man had enough sense to accept a job with lower salary...*so that he could learn from the very best.*

Learning from the Best may necessitate a geographical change. You might have to move from where you are to another state. *Do it, if that is what it takes.*

Remember the true reason is you are there *to learn.*

Remember the specific knowledge you are trying to learn. If you are sitting at the feet of a great electrician, he may know little about protocol. But, you are not there to learn about protocol. You are there to learn about electricity.

You won't learn everything from one person during your life. Don't attempt it. It is too much stress on them. You will be disappointed. God never intended for you to do so. *Many* are necessary to make you successful, learned and skilled throughout your life.

Always sit at the feet of the Best.

It's one of the Secrets of the Journey.

≈ 4 ≈
ALWAYS KEEP A BOOK
ACCESSIBLE FOR READING

Make Moments Count.
Always keep a book with you.
What you read is what you will become.

Reading prevents boredom. That is why magazines and books are kept in the waiting rooms of physicians and hospitals. When you bring the book of your choice with you, you can maintain a *continuous* flow of *appropriate* information into your heart and mind.

Reading discourages others from beginning an unproductive conversation with you. Have you ever sat beside someone who could not stop talking? Unfortunately, most people who love to talk a lot do not require anything significant to energize them. They will talk about anything just to avoid silence. Your book discourages them.

Keep a list of the books you want to read each month. Everyone should read at least one book a week. (At the beginning of each year select 52 books that you would like to complete by the end of the year.)

Bring books with you on airplane trips and vacations. You are away from the busyness of your daily schedule, the phone, and the television. You can withdraw into your own private mental world. Focus is now possible.

Keep reading material in your washroom. Avoid two-year-old magazines that do not keep you current and energized. Place books there that are a priority for you. Keep a Bible there.

Keep two books in your automobile at all times. I suggest keeping a fiction book and a nonfiction book simultaneously. Moods vary. Sometimes, you want to *relax.* Other times you will want to *learn.* Keep *both* convenient. During traffic jams, this relieves the stress of "doing nothing" en route to an appointment.

Make books accessible to others riding with you as well. This reading habit helps them focus, too. *Your life stays on course.*

My life is quite full. There is little time for loneliness, self pity or "down time." *Every moment matters to me.* Every hour matters to me. That's why keeping a book handy is so advantageous.

Your needs continuously change. Familiarize yourself with the rhythms of your day and your personal life. Cooperate with them and you can become more productive than you really realized.

Do not to fight against the surge of energy in your life, but rather flow with it and make every moment count.

Reading books in those moments *does wonders.* *It's one of the Secrets of the Journey.*

⤳ 5 ⤳

AVOID QUESTIONS THAT FUEL CONFUSION

━━━━━━➤☰-✪-☰◀━━━━━━

Remember, Satan Asked The First Question.

So ask the right questions. Accept the fact...you are not God. That's why the apostle Paul wrote to his protégé, "But foolish and unlearned questions avoid, knowing that they do gender strifes," (2 Timothy 2:23).

I have a tenacious curiosity. My mind is in constant pursuit of answers and solutions. Now, there is nothing really wrong with desiring answers. Everyone knows that. But ask *appropriate* questions.

You see, it was a *simple question* in the beautiful Garden of Eden *that birthed the greatest tragedy* that has ever occurred in the life of man.

Satan asked the first question on record, "Now the serpent was more subtil than any beast of the field which the Lord God had made. And he said unto the woman, Yea, hath God said, Ye shall not eat of every tree of the garden?" (Genesis 3:1). He set the trap.

Doubt was the bait.

Eve fell for it. Adam followed. You and I have paid a dear price for their tragic mistakes.

Always ask the questions God likes to answer.

The obedient ask, "*What* must I do?"

The disobedient ask, "*Why* should I do it?"

Stop asking questions others are unqualified to answer. I remember sitting around a table asking stupid questions such as, "Which came first, the chicken or the egg?" In my early ministry, I remember sitting on a Greyhound bus trying to answer a question from a cynical old man, "Who did Cain marry?" What a waste of time!

Laugh at the attempts of cynics to intimidate you with difficult questions. Don't get angry. You see, the cynic is not living the answers he already knows in his heart. He is using questions *as a smoke screen* to distract you from his own rebellion. The Pharisees tried this. Jesus moved *away* from them and went home with Zacchaeus, who recognized his need of Jesus.

Stop asking unanswerable questions about Divine healing. One of the greatest and most effective men in our generation is Oral Roberts. Once, he said, "I can't figure out healing. I pray for some I don't think will be healed, and God heals them. I pray for others I just know will be healed, and they don't receive it. *It's all still a mystery to me.*"

You see, He doesn't play God.

Don't try to explain tragedies. Nobody can fully explain why someone is healed and another dies. My own parents cannot explain the death of two of their children. But they have embraced the goodness of God and the "evilness" of satan. God gives life, and satan takes life. "The thief cometh not, but for to steal, and to kill, and to destroy: I am come that they might have life, and that they might have it more abundantly," (John 10:10). Thousands leave the Highway of Answers to build their entire conversation around the pothole of questions.

You can't climb mountains studying pebbles.

Ask appropriate questions from proven leaders. Many young ministers sit at banquets next to remarkable pastors without asking one single question of advice or correction.

Keep your microcassette available for documenting answers to your questions. Don't trust your memory. I keep a recorder in my hand or pocket continually. When I ask questions, I can't risk forgetting the answers.

Don't attempt to ask brilliant questions. You will end up looking like a fool. The best way to impress others is not to try. *Be genuine* about the answers you are pursuing.

Handling improper questions is important.

Often, after delivering some of the most powerful Wisdom Keys on success, I have been approached by someone who ignored everything taught that night. They had searched for one possible question that would "stump me." In my beginning years, I thought they were sincere. I wasted hundreds of hours in my early ministry trying to become "The Answer Man" to everybody. It was ridiculous! (Don't try to know everything in life. Strive to know the most important things.)

Now, this is what I do:

1.   *Pray a prayer of faith* for them that The Holy Spirit will begin to dominate and rule their life.

2.   *Recommend to them* a Wisdom Book that I

have already written.

    3.   *Invite them to invest* in a Wisdom Pak of Tapes that could revolutionize their lives.

    4.   *Evaluate their response.* Their response to my suggestions reveals the depth of their true appetite for Wisdom. Time-wasters are everywhere. I meet them daily. Time is the most precious gift I have, and I refuse to permit a cynic or a fool to destroy it.

Stop asking and answering foolish questions.

It's one of the most important Secrets of the Journey.

⮊ 6 ⮌
REMEMBER THAT GOD SEES SOMETHING IN YOU THAT OTHERS DO NOT SEE

Something Incredible Is Inside You.
Your *Assignment* was decided in your mother's womb. "Before I formed thee in the belly I knew thee; and before thou camest forth out of the womb I sanctified thee, and I ordained thee a prophet unto the nations," (Jeremiah 1:5). God knows it. He created you. He has known the invisible purpose for which you were created.

You are not an accident waiting to happen. "I will praise Thee; for I am fearfully and wonderfully made: marvellous are Thy works; and that my soul knoweth right well," (Psalm 139:14).

Everything inside you is known, treasured and intended for full use by your Creator. "My substance was not hid from Thee, when I was made in secret, and curiously wrought in the lowest parts of the earth," (Psalm 139:15).

Your flaws do not necessarily prevent God from using you. They exist to motivate your pursuit of Him. "Thine eyes did see my substance, yet being unperfect; and in Thy book all my members were written, which in continuance were fashioned, when as yet there was none of them," (Psalm 139:16).

Your very existence excites God. "How precious also are Thy thoughts unto me, O God! how great is the sum of them! If I should count them, they are more in number than the sand: when I awake, I am still with Thee," (Psalm 139:17-18).

Picture an author exultant over his book. The book exists. The author created it. He is excited about it whether anyone else is or not. Imagine a composer, exhilarated over a completed song. He knew its beginning and its ending. Its very presence excites him.

Your very presence energizes God. He saw your beginning and the desired conclusion. "For Thou hast created all things, and for Thy pleasure they are and were created," (Revelation 4:11).

God is looking at something within you *that you have never seen.* "For man looketh on the outward appearance, but the Lord looketh on the heart," (1 Samuel 16:7).

God is looking at something inside you *satan cannot even discern.* "Lest satan should get an advantage of us: for we are not ignorant of his devices," (2 Corinthians 2:11).

God is looking at something you contain that *you have not yet discovered.* "For as the Heavens are higher than the earth, so are My ways higher than your ways, and My thoughts than your thoughts," (Isaiah 55:9).

God will tell you secrets satan will never hear.

His mercies are not wasted on you. He has big plans. His forgiveness is not futile. You are becoming a monument and trophy of His grace. "For we are His workmanship, created in Christ Jesus unto good works," (Ephesians 2:10).

God boasts about you to every demon (Job 1:8).

You may be looking at your *beginning*.

God is looking at your *end*.

You may be obsessed with your *flaws*.

God is obsessed with your *future*.

You may be focusing on your *enemies*.

God is focusing on your *eventuality*.

God is not *awaiting* your becoming. He is awaiting your *discovery* of it.

So never consult those who have not discovered what is within you. Their focus is different. Their conclusions are inaccurate.

Stay in the presence of the One who created you. You will always feel confident about yourself when you stay in His presence. He is looking at something in you that is remarkable. He planted it within you while you were yet in your mother's womb.

David understood this. King Saul and his brothers saw brashness; The Holy Spirit saw *boldness*. His brothers saw anger; God saw a sense of justice.

Joseph understood this. His brothers saw pride. God saw *thankfulness*. The brothers saw rivalry; God saw a *weapon*.

That's why the opinions and observations of others are not your foundation for greatness. Stop pursuing their conclusions. God is looking at something inside you they *cannot see, refuse* to see and may *never see*.

The brothers of Jesus did not grasp His *divinity*.

The brothers of Joseph *misinterpreted him*.

The brothers of David saw a mere shepherd boy.

The friends of Job could not discern the satanic scenario *before his crisis.*

Haman could not even discern the nationality of Esther!

Few are ever accurate in their assessment of you. *Few.*

Your flaws are *much less* than they imagine.

Your greatness is *far greater* than they discern.

The Holy Spirit is the only One who has accurately assessed your *future,* your *ingredients* and the *willingness* of your heart to become great. That's why He keeps reaching, pursuing and developing you in the midst of every attack and crisis.

He never *gives up* on you.

He never *quits looking at you.*

He never *changes His plans* toward you.

He never quits believing in your future.

He has decided the conclusion and is only awaiting your discovery of it.

Remember this continuously. God is seeing something inside you that keeps Him excited and involved. "Then Samuel took the horn of oil, and anointed him in the midst of his brethren: and the Spirit of the Lord came upon David from that day forward," (1 Samuel 16:13).

It's one of the golden Secrets of the Journey.

7

SOW YOUR SEED WITH EXPECTATION OF A HARVEST

You Can Only Do What You Know.

Thousands have been taught that it is wrong to expect something in return when you give something to God.

They feel that this is proof of greed.

"When I give to God, I expect nothing in return!" is the prideful claim of many who have been taught this terrible error.

Do you *expect* something from your boss at the end of a work week? Of course.

Did you *expect* forgiveness when you confessed your sins to Christ? Of course.

I want to show you how stripping expectation from your Seed is *theft of the only pleasure God knows.* You see, God's greatest need is to believed. His greatest pain is to be doubted. "But without faith it is impossible to please Him: for he that cometh to God must believe that He is, and that He is a rewarder," (Hebrews 11:6).

Motive means *reason for doing something.*

When someone on trial is accused of a murder, they try to find the motive or reason why he would do such a horrible thing.

God gave us a Harvest as a reason for sowing Seed. He expected us to be motivated by supply, the promise of provision. "Give, and it shall be given unto you; good measure, pressed down, and shaken together, and running over, shall men give into your bosom," (Luke 6:38).

He offers overflow *as a reason* for sowing Seed. Seeds of forgiveness or whatever you need. "Honour the Lord with thy substance, and with the firstfruits of all thine increase: So shall thy barns be filled with plenty, and thy presses shall burst out with new wine," (Proverbs 3:9-10).

Notice that He paints the picture of overflowing barns to motivate us *(give us a reason for)* honoring Him.

The reason to sow is so clear. "Bring ye all the tithes into the storehouse, that there may be meat in Mine house, and prove Me now herewith, saith the Lord of hosts, if I will not open you the windows of Heaven, and pour you out a blessing, that there shall not be room enough to receive it," (Malachi 3:10).

Read Deuteronomy 28:1-14. Here in Scripture God creates a list of the specific blessings that will occur if you obey Him. Why does He give us these portraits of prosperity? To inspire and give us a *reason for obedience.*

Peter needed this kind of encouragement just like you and I do today. He felt such self-pity as he related to Christ that he and the others had "given up everything." Jesus promises an hundredfold return. "But he shall receive an hundredfold now in this time," (Mark 10:30).

Many people think it is evil to sow for a Harvest. Absurdity. That is the reason to sow!

Giving is the *cure* for greed, not hoarding. When you sow to get a Harvest, you have just mastered greed. Greed hoards. Man withholds. Satan steals.

The nature of God alone is the giving nature. When you *give,* you have just revealed the nature of God *inside you.*

The only pleasure God receives is through acts of faith. His only *need* is to be believed. His *greatest* need is to be believed. "God is not a man, that He should lie," (Numbers 23:19).

When Jesus talked to the woman at the well of Samaria, He promised her water that she would never thirst again. Was that wrong to offer her something if she pursued Him? Of course not. That was the purpose of the portrait of water—to motivate her and give her a *reason* for obeying Him.

Somebody counted 470 papaya seeds in a single papaya. If that was consistent, one papaya seed will produce a plant containing ten papayas. If each of the ten contained 470 seeds, there would be 4,700 papaya seeds on one plant. Now, just suppose you replant those 4,700 seeds to create 4,700 more plants. Do you know how much 5,000 plants containing 5,000 seeds would be? Twenty-five million seeds... on the second planting alone.

Yet, we still have difficulty over really believing in the hundred-fold return.

Millions must *unlearn* the poisonous and traitorous teaching that it is wrong to expect anything in return.

Expectation is the powerful current that makes the Seed work for you. "But without faith it is impossible to please Him: for he that cometh to God must believe that He is, and that He is a rewarder of them that diligently seek Him," (Hebrews 11:6).

Expect protection as He promised. "And I will rebuke the devourer for your sakes, and he shall not destroy the fruits of your ground; neither shall your vine cast her fruit before the time in the field, saith the Lord of hosts," (Malachi 3:11).

Expect favor from a Boaz close to you. "Give, and it shall be given unto you; good measure, pressed down, and shaken together, and running over, shall men give into your bosom. For with the same measure that ye mete withal it shall be measured to you again," (Luke 6:38).

Expect financial ideas and Wisdom from God as a Harvest. "But thou shalt remember the Lord thy God: for it is He that giveth thee power to get wealth," (Deuteronomy 8:18).

Expect your enemies to fragment and be confused and flee before you. "The Lord shall cause thine enemies that rise up against thee to be smitten before thy face: they shall come out against thee one way, and flee before thee seven ways," (Deuteronomy 28:7).

Expect God to bless you for every act of obedience. "...if thou shalt hearken diligently unto the voice of the Lord...And all these blessings shall come on thee," (Deuteronomy 28:1-2).

Always sow with great expectation.

It's one of the Secrets of the Journey.

DECISION

Will You Accept Jesus As Your Personal Savior Today?

The Bible says, "That if thou shalt confess with thy mouth the Lord Jesus, and shalt believe in thine heart that God hath raised Him from the dead, thou shalt be saved," (Romans 10:9).

Pray this prayer from your heart today!

"Dear Jesus, I believe that You died for me and rose again on the third day. I confess I am a sinner...I need Your love and forgiveness...Come into my heart. Forgive my sins. I receive Your eternal life. Confirm Your love by giving me peace, joy and supernatural love for others. Amen."

DR. MIKE MURDOCK

is in tremendous demand as one of the most dynamic speakers in America today.

More than 17,000 audiences in over 100 countries have attended his Schools of Wisdom and conferences. Hundreds of invitations come to him from churches, colleges and business corporations. He is a noted author of over 250 books, including the best sellers, *The Leadership Secrets of Jesus* and *Secrets of the Richest Man Who Ever Lived.* Thousands view his weekly television program, *Wisdom Keys with Mike Murdock.* Many attend his Schools of Wisdom that he hosts in many cities of America.

☐ Yes, Mike, I made a decision to accept Christ as my personal Savior today. Please send me my free gift of your book, *31 Keys to a New Beginning* to help me with my new life in Christ. *(B-48)*

NAME   BIRTHDAY

ADDRESS

CITY   STATE   ZIP

PHONE   E-MAIL

Mail to: **The Wisdom Center** · 4051 Denton Hwy. · Ft. Worth, TX 76117
1-817-759-BOOK · 1-817-759-0300
You Will Love Our Website..! WisdomOnline.com

JOIN THE
Wisdom Key 3000
TODAY!

Will You Become My Ministry Partner In The Work of God?

Dear Friend,

God has connected us!

I have asked The Holy Spirit for 3000 Special Partners who will plant a monthly Seed of $58.00 to help me bring the gospel around the world. (58 represents 58 kinds of blessings in the Bible.)

Will you become my monthly Faith Partner in The Wisdom Key 3000? Your monthly Seed of $58.00 is so powerful in helping heal broken lives. When you sow into the work of God, 4 Miracle Harvests are guaranteed in Scripture, Isaiah 58...

- ► Uncommon Health (Isaiah 58)
- ► Uncommon Wisdom For Decision-Making (Isaiah 58)
- ► Uncommon Financial Favor (Isaiah 58)
- ► Uncommon Family Restoration (Isaiah 58)

Your Faith Partner,

Mike Murdock

P.S. Please clip the coupon attached and return it to me today, so I can rush the Wisdom Key Partnership Pak to you...or call me at 1-817-759-0300.